378783

Maths at Work

Maths at the Vet's

Tracey Steffora

Raintree is an imprint of Capstone Global Library Limited, a company incorporated in England and Wales having its registered office at 7 Pilgrim Street, London, EC4V 6LB – Registered company number: 6695582

To contact Raintree please phone 0845 6044371, fax + 44 (0) 1865 312263, or email myorders@ raintreepublishers.co.uk. Customers from outside the UK please telephone +44 1865 312262.

Text © Capstone Global Library Limited 2013
First published in hardback in 2013
The moral rights of the proprietor have been asserted.

Edited by Dan Nunn and Abby Colich
Designed by Victoria Allen
Picture research by Tracy Cummins
Production control by Victoria Fitzgerald
Printed and bound in China by Leo Paper Products Ltd

ISBN 978 1 406 25075 6
16 15 14 13 12
10 9 8 7 6 5 4 3 2 1

British Library Cataloguing in Publication Data
Steffora, Tracey.
Maths at the vet's. – (Maths at work)
510-dc23
A full catalogue record for this book is available from the British Library.

Acknowledgements
We would like to thank the following for permission to reproduce photographs: Corbis: pp. 7 (© Ocean), 11 (© Corbis); Getty Images: pp. 5 (John Wood Photography), 12 (Michael Urban/AFP), 15 (Vstock LLC), 18 (John Wood Photography), 19 (Thinkstock), 20 (LWA); iStockphoto: pp. 4 (© kali9), 14 (© Alina Solovyova-Vincent), 16 (© Miodrag Gajic), 22b (© Alina Solovyova-Vincent); Shutterstock: pp. 6 (Eric Isselée), 8 (Vladislav Pavlovich), 10 (Mark William Penny), 13 (Pixel Memoirs), 17 (Utekhina Anna), 22a (erashov); Superstock: pp. 9 (© Minden Pictures), 21 (© Kablonk).

Front cover photograph of a vet examining a bulldog puppy reproduced with permission from Getty Images (Photographer's Choice).

Back cover photograph of a vet with a ferret reproduced with permission from Shutterstock (Vladislav Pavlovich).

Every effort has been made to contact copyright holders of any material reproduced in this book. Any omissions will be rectified in subsequent printings if notice is given to the publisher.

Contents

Maths at the vet's

A vet is a doctor for animals.

A vet uses maths every day.

Size

Animals are different sizes.

This animal is big.

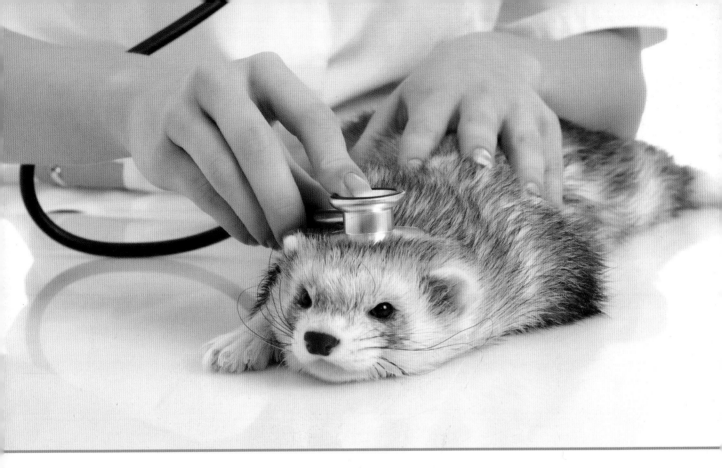

This animal is small.

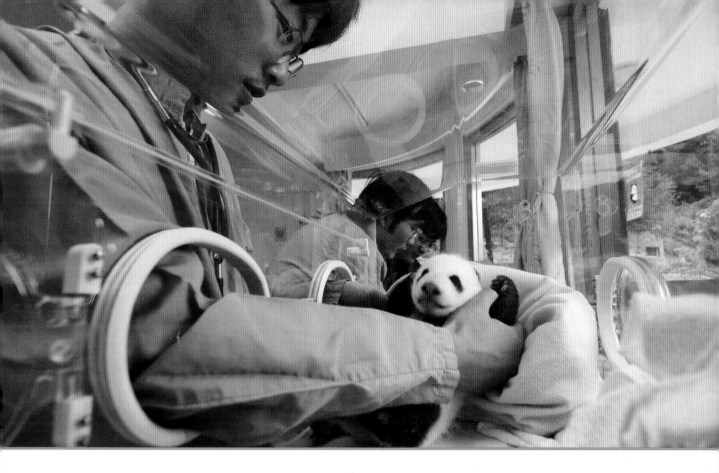

Is this animal big or small?

(answer on page 22)

Measuring

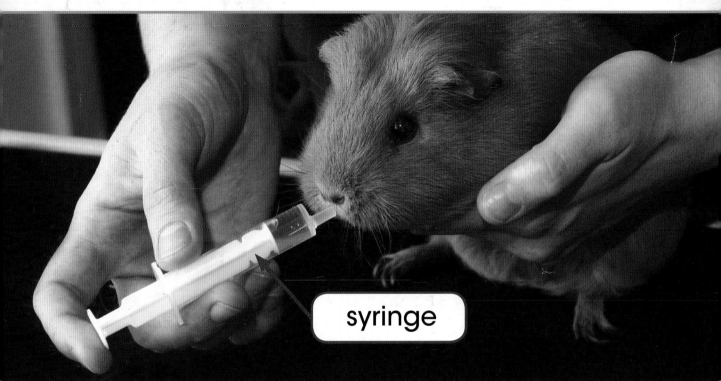

syringe

The vet measures how much medicine to give an animal.

scales

The vet measures how heavy an animal is.

The vet measures how long an animal is.

Which is taller? The cat or the dog?

(answer on page 22)

13

Counting

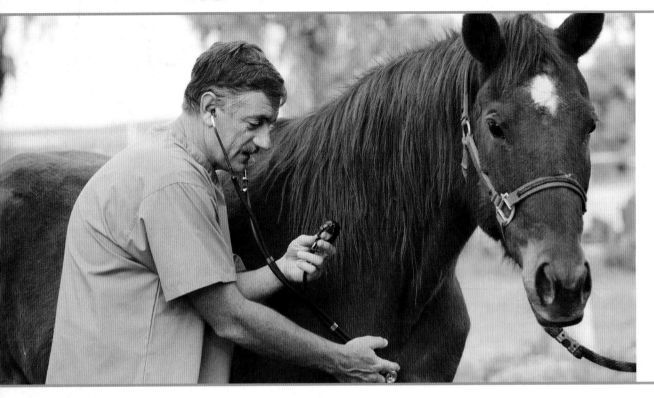

The vet counts heartbeats.

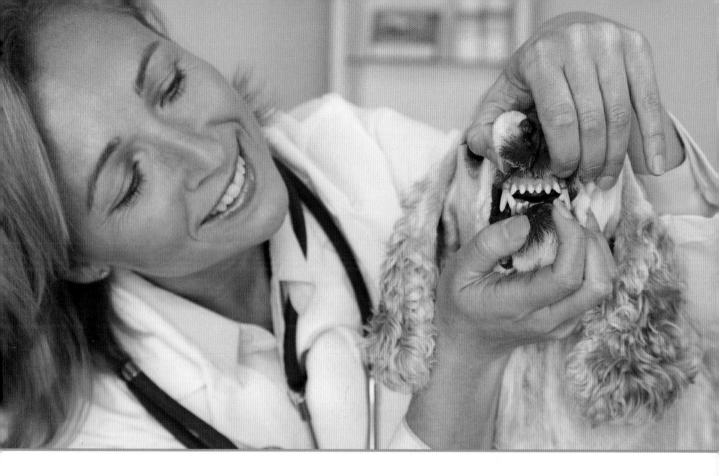

The vet counts teeth.

The vet counts puppies.

How many kittens are there?

(answer on page 22)

Time

The vet sees many animals
each day.

The vet sees one animal at a time.

clock

A clock shows what time it is.

Schedule

Time	Name	Animal
8.00 a.m.	Rover	dog
8.30 a.m.	Fluffy	cat
9.00 a.m.	Patches	rabbit
9.30 a.m.	Bob	cat

What time will the vet see Fluffy?

(answer on page 22)

Answers

page 9: The animal is small.

page 13: The dog is taller.

page 17: There are five kittens.

page 21: The vet will see Fluffy at 8.30 a.m. (a.m. means in the morning).

Picture glossary

clock object used for measuring and telling the time

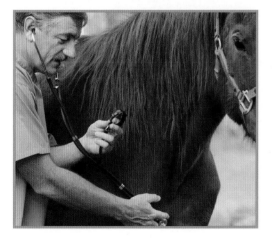

heartbeat sound that happens when the heart pumps blood

Index

Notes for parents and teachers
Maths is a way that we make sense of the world around us. For the young child, this includes recognizing similarities and differences, classifying objects, recognizing shapes and patterns, developing number sense, and using simple measurement skills.

Before reading
Connect with what children know
Discuss what a vet does and allow children to share any experience they have had caring for animals or taking animals to the vet's surgery.

After reading
Build upon children's curiosity and desire to explore
- Identify some of the different tools that a vet uses, such as scales, stethoscope, thermometer, and ruler. Discuss what these tools measure, and ask children to look through other books about vets to identify pictures of these tools being used.
- Ask the children to name animals they are familiar with. Ask questions that encourage comparison such as: "Which is taller, a cow or a chicken?" and "Do you think a cat or a horse has a longer tail?"